The SIN

A HUMOROUS LOOK AT RUGBY LEAGUE

By
**Steve Spencer,
Peter Hardy
& Dave Farrar**

London League Publications Ltd

The Sin Bin
A HUMOROUS LOOK AT RUGBY LEAGUE

A CIP catalogue record for this book is available from the British Library.

First published in Great Britain in October 1996 by:

London League Publications Ltd.
P. O. Box 10441
London E14 0SB

ISBN 0 9526064 1 0

Design by:
Steve Spencer, Caricatures & Illustrations
12 Yardley Way, Bradford BD12 0JF

Printed and bound by:
Juma Printing & Publishing
44 Wellington Street, Sheffield S1 4HD

About the Authors

Steven A. Spencer: Graduated with Honours in Fine Art at The Polytechnic Wolverhampton [now University] in 1987, and has since worked in catalogue production for Empire Stores. Steve also works as a freelance illustrator and his work has appeared in *League Express, League Express Weekend, Super League Week*, IPC Magazines, *Cycle Sport, Total Sport* and various other publications. Since 1991 he has designed and produced the cover artwork for *TGG! (The Greatest Game!)* not to mention supplying numerous illustrations.

Peter Hardy: Bradford born Peter Hardy saw his first Rugby League match in 1973. He was so impressed that only 10 years later he went to see another. Since then he has seen several more, including that now legendary encounter, frequently described as the greatest of the century, between Trafford Borough and Runcorn Highfield. He is the life president and sole member of the Yorkshire branch of the Shaun Edwards Appreciation Society, and in his spare time edits the Rugby League Supporters Association magazine *The Greatest Game!*

Dave Farrar: Responsible for the "Life Down South Cartoons", and the text for Karl Harrison. Dave has watched Rugby League for more than 30 years. He draws regularly and writes for *London Calling!*, the Broncos fanzine, and is a member of its editorial board. He was also one of the joint authors of *Touch and Go- a history of professional Rugby League in London*, and *I Wouldn't Start From Here- a travelling supporters guide to British Rugby League grounds*. He currently works in local government administration.

Special Thanks To:

Peter Lush: Who coordinated the book for London League Publications Ltd. This involved worrying a lot, and encouraging and nagging the authors.

Michael O'Hare: Who proof read the book and offered advice and support.

Nigel Wilde: For "The Flatcappers". Nigel also contributes work to various fanzines including *The Greatest Game*.

John Wood: Like the sub who comes off the bench to score the winning try, John's valuable text inputting services helped us meet the print deadline!
John also compiles and produces the Sin Bin pages for *The Greatest Game*.

Jonathan Coleman: For being a great sport and writing the preface for the book. Page 3.

Lol Ferrier: For "Tarquin The Scoreboard". Page 87.

Andrew Griffiths: For "The Adventures of The Ed" From South Wales *Rebel Rugby* fanzine. Page 98.

Stephen McCarthy: For "And I say the reindeer were off side" cartoon. Page 22.

Acknowledgements:

Thanks to Grandstand Publications for permission to use the quotation on page 24 from *The Official Rugby League Centenary Magazine*. Colin Welland's article on Brian Bevan.

Some illustrations previously published in *League Express*, *The Greatest Game* and *London Calling!*

Scripts to the first 4 "Flatcappers" in order of appearance are credited to Stuart Lake of the R.L.S.A.

"Now then Will... A player of your standard should fit in well here!"

Preface:

Virgin Radio's Jonathan Coleman - Live from The Sin Bin

Footy is all about having fun. If a player loses his shorts when being tackled, or a guy drops the ball over the line it gets a laugh. Who hasn't laughed at the overweight prop forward or the dog that runs onto the pitch and can't be chased off? To most League fans both here and in Oz, the fate of our team is of critical importance. A bad defeat can put that little black cloud over our week, especially for us Broncos fans. If we can't find something to laugh at in the game, it's a poor show. Some of the refs I see in England could be described as laughable (but enough of my problems)... "I still reckon it was a try."

I hope this book is a big success as the game is a great institution, but the humorous side of the thing is often missed by League writers . Cartoons can capture the essential good nature of the game and those little incidents that you can laugh about in the bar and recall years later. Rugby has its own world of gags and bizarre situations that sometimes only a cartoonist can encapsulate. It's about time that the fun side of the game was put into print. League is full of characters and most of these have been captured by the blokes who've put together *The Sin Bin*.

At the end of each Rugby League game, both teams and fans have a beer in the bar afterwards, and have a joke about what's gone on. This book attempts to recreate that atmosphere, as opposed to soccer where they beat each other up after the game, In League, the players just do it during the game!

It has been a pleasure to be part of this book. I hope it does well, even though I won't get a cent as usual!

Happy tackling.

Up the Broncos

Jonathan Coleman

(The Russ and Jono Show)

Jeff Grayshon MBE

Appearance: The man who came to fix the plumbing at Mount Pleasant but got drafted onto the subs' bench to make up the numbers.

Why was he really there? Jeff's the veteran player who turned coach in 1995 to lead Batley back into the First Division.

Veteran. In Rugby League that means he's about 32 doesn't it? Not in this case. Jeff is a proper veteran of 47.

I don't wish to be ageist, but isn't that knocking on a bit for a sportsman? Well, it does make him the oldest professional Rugby League player ever (easily beating Joe Ferguson who was 44 years and 48 days old when he played for Oldham against St Helens in 1923).

I presume he's been playing a while then? Well, those not even born when Jeff made his debut in 1969 include Phil Clarke, Jason Robinson, Paul Newlove, Alan Hunte and Bobbie Goulding.

I think I get the idea. Who did he play for? Broughton Rangers? Fleetwood Northern Union? Ironically, given the team he coached, it was their great local rivals Dewsbury, where he was part of the team that beat Leeds in the Championship final back in 1973. Sadly though, his playing career was cut short by a knee injury and he turned to coaching.

That was quite recent then? No, that was back in 1978. His injury wasn't as bad as everyone thought and he began to turn out for Dewsbury again. This led to his signing by high flying Bradford Northern (now Bulls), get your head around that concept, and his first Great Britain cap the following year, 1979. In 1982 he was appointed GB captain and, in 1985, aged 36 years and 8 months, he became Britain's oldest ever Test player.

So how long does he intend to continue playing? As long as his knee lets him, probably. Jeff once said that if he could get a new leg he'd play until he was 50 (or 60 with his existing leg if he converted to Union!).

What's his style as a coach? Surprisingly, given the amount of time he spent following Peter Fox around, playing for him at Bradford (twice), Leeds and Featherstone, he hasn't yet taken to wearing baseball caps or flicking "V" signs at the crowd! He has, however, got Foxy's way with a quote, modestly saying after their Challenge Cup match against the then World Champions from Central Park that if Batley couldn't beat Wigan, no one could!

Not to be confused with: Paul Grayshon (his son who plays for Rochdale Hornets); Larry Grayson; Harry Gration; Geoff Fletcher; George Foreman; Methuselah (the oldest guy in the Bible, you ignorant lot!).

Least likely to say: "It's a young man's game."

Most likely to say: "So Paul Junior, what's it like playing against your Grandad?"

FOX'S

MOUNT PLEASANT

FOX'S

BATLEY R.L.F.C. PRIDE & HERITAGE

5

The Flat Cappers

by Wilde

Shaun Edwards OBE

Description: Mean, moody and MAGNIFICENT!

Pardon? We are talking about the same Shaun Edwards, aren't we? The one with a face like a bulldog that's been licking chilli off a thistle? (or a bulldog chewing a wasp!) We are indeed. Wigan's mid field maestro is one of the treasures of Rugby League and should be treated as such.

Surely you jest? Listen the pie-eaters know a good player when they see one and they've held on to this one for 12 years. He may not be as eye-catching as Robinson, as fast as Offiah or as scary as Tuigamala but he hasn't got more winner's medals than any other player by being rubbish.

Well I suppose he's all right but he's useless against the Aussies. Oh I don't know, played 10, won 6 is a good a record as any other British player of his generation (that's three World club Challenges and three test matches). However, it's not just for his playing skills that all League fans should love him. He's one of RL's most complex and interesting personalities.

He never looks very complex. Look at the facts (he once allegedly refused to shake John Major's hand on the grounds that the government's policies had made so many of his friends unemployed). His favourite TV programmes are current affairs documentaries but he prefers reading biographies to watching TV (which in sporting terms makes him an intellectual). He is known for his ferocious will to win but is also a regular church goer.

So he's a sort of cross between Vlad the Impaler and Thora Hird? Very funny. He's probably also the first Rugby League player to go out with a pop star (if you discount the rumours about Brian Bevan and Alma Cogan), the pop star in question being Heather Small of the Mercury Music Prize winning M People.

I can just see Shaun rubbing shoulders with Jarvis Cocker and the mad bloke out of the Prodigy. Well that's one of the perks of being a pop superstar these days. You get to rub shoulders with Wigan players. However the greatest reason for clasping Shaun to our collective bosoms is that Shaun will never be a "Rugby" player, always a Rugby League player.

I'm afraid you've lost me here. Remember Wigan's matches against rugby union opposition? For Shaun (and apparently Shaun alone) these weren't just money making exercises or applications for off season employment. For him it was a chance to settle the scores after a hundred years of prejudice and injustice. After trouncing the cream of union at the Middlesex Sevens he took great delight in announcing that Wigan weren't even RL's best team, St Helens were! No one really believed he thought this was true but the point was made. Shaun is a Rugby League man.

Not to be confused with: Diccon Edwards; Jimmy Edwards; Percy Edwards; Will Carling.

Low points of his career in the eyes of others: Being sent off against the Australians in 1992; the Centenary Season's blond rinse.

THE REAL ENGLAND CAPTAIN

9

WIRE V PARIS

WIRE V PARIS

WIRE V PARIS

Laurie Daley

Description: Former future captain of Australia.

Laurie... that's a girl's name isn't it? No, you're thinking of Laura. Laurie is definitely a boy, and he's got the stubble and hairy legs to prove it.

So has my Aunt Glenda... Less of the ITV style humour please. We're talking about one of Australia's finest here. Laurie's generally regarded as one of the best players in the world, although in which position seems to be a bit controversial. In Great Britain he's regarded as the finest stand - off half in the world, while the Australians think he's the world's greatest five-eighth whatever one of those is.

So tell me all about Laura... I mean Laurie: Laurie's a country boy from the town of Junee (you must know it. On the road between Wagga Wagga and Cootamundra, just above the Murrumbidgee river. You'll have passed it loads of times). He joined the Canberra Raiders back in 1987 but first came to British attention in the 1990 Ashes series.

Did he make an impact on British Rugby League? Well he did in one sense. He made the team as a replacement for Wally Lewis, He'd been left behind with a controversial broken arm (Wally said it was fixed. no one else agreed), so it was all a bit ironic when Laurie broke his hand in a punch up at Headingley and missed the first test.

So you could say he was a "big hit": Listen, I'm warning you. If you want to be Shane Ritchie do it in your own time. Anyway, Laurie was well enough to bedevil us in the second and third tests, and has been doing so ever since. In total he's played in 19 tests and captained Australia in the absence of Mal Meninga in the first test of the Trans-Tasman series in 1993. On the domestic front, he's played in three Premiership victories for Canberra (1989, 90 & 94) and led New South Wales to three consecutive State of Origin victories (1992, 93 & 94).

So, presumably he played a big part in Australia's 1995 World Cup victory? Actually he played no part in it at all. Canberra were one of the prime movers of Super League and their players, including Laurie, signed up for it en masse. Therefore the ARL refused to select any of them for the national team. They were also excluded from the 1995 State of Origin matches. This actually had a beneficial effect on Canberra who, with none of their players away on representative duty, lost only three times all season. Laurie in particular had a good season, winning numerous Player of the Year awards.

So Laurie is a Super League man? Oh yes. He appeared on adverts promoting it and, at the height of the court, case announced that he'd rather play Aussie Rules than ever play for the ARL again.

So where is he now? Er... playing for the ARL again actually. Although Canberra forfeited their first match of the season by not turning out, they're now playing like they mean it and should be on course for a play-off place. Meanwhile a Super League truce allowed players from both camps to take part in the 1996 State of Origin which Laurie's NSW won with a clean sweep, the first since 1986. What happens on the international front still depends on the result of the upcoming court case but do not be surprised if Laurie is seen wearing green and gold again some time soon. He may even be the future captain again.

Not to be confused with: Arthur Daley, Dally Messenger, Daily Mail, Laura Ashley.

Most likely to say: "Of course when I said 'never', what I actually meant was..."

"This Super League will be the death of t'owd flat

The Further Adventures of Mo   by Spencer

TER-MO-NATOR

During 1993 Maurice Lindsay
presided over some very unpopular changes! The return to
two divisions and the expulsions of Chorley, Nottingham and
Blackpool were two of them!

15

Andy Gregory

Description: Pocket - sized national hero.

Why what's he done to deserve the thanks of a grateful nation?
Andy helped guarantee a pie - eaters free Wembley for the first time
since 1987 when his Salford team knocked Wigan out of the Challenge
Cup. Admittedly the nation was at its most grateful around the St Helens
area but most of Rugby League thought it was about time the ribbons on
the cup were changed to a different colour.

Andy's a Wigan lad isn't he? It's a bit ironic him ending their cup run.
In many ways Andy was the typical eighties Wigan player. He was a big
name signing from another club (like Ellery Hanley, Joe Lydon, Kelvin
Skerrett, Andy Goodway, Andy Platt , etc), who then went on to play for
Leeds (like Ellery, Andy, Kevin Iro, Bobbie Goulding, etc) and later became
a coach (Like Ellery, Andy, Kevin, Joe, Graham West and Ian Lucas).

**Hold on, what was that about him being a big name signing? I thought
he was a local lad?** He was. He played for Wigan St Pats and won the
BARLA Young Player of the Year in 1978, but Wigan didn't sign local lads
back then so he went elsewhere. He had a trial for Salford but didn't sign
for them because his dad didn't get on with the then coach, Alex Murphy.
He eventually joined Widnes when, after the departure of Reg Bowden
to Fulham, he became the regular scrum - half. In 1985 he moved on to
Warrington and when he did eventually join Wigan in 1987 he cost them
a then record £130,000.

Worth the money? Well he won the award for First Division Player of the
Year in his first season at Central Park and Wigan began their residency at
Wembley so you decide.

If a thing's worth doing, it's worth doing twice. Andy is only the second
person to win the Lance Todd Trophy twice (1988 and 1990). He's also
probably the only coach to win the First (nee Second) Division Championship
two seasons on the trot with the same team; firstly the promotion-free Centenary
Season and then the inaugural summer season later the same year.

Just how little is "Little" Andy Gregory? At only 5'4" Andy is the same
height as "Little" Roger Millward but slightly shorter than "Little" Peter
Sterling (5'5"). "Little" Deryck Fox is 5'6" while "Little" Bobbie Goulding
at 5'8" isn't really "little" at all, although "Average - sized" Bobbie Goulding
probably wouldn't roll off Ray French's tongue as easily. However all of
the team are bigger than pop's "purple pixie" Prince (or is it Symbol)?
who is a whopping 5'1".

Great unexplained mysteries: Is gravity stronger around the Salford area?
Andy definitely seems to be getting shorter and wider. Or perhaps he's
just hanging around with taller people these days.

Not to be confused with: Mike Gregory, Glen Gregory, Gregory Peck,
Napoleon Bonaparte (as far as we know that "Petite General" rode
a horse, not a Harley Davidson).

8th May 1996
WIGAN 82
BATH   6

PORKIES PIES

Shirt Tales

by Spencer

Winter Rugby League in Britain

SPLAT!!

Summer Rugby League in Britain

SPLAT!!

Lee Crooks

Description: The Rugby League fan's Rugby League player.

Er, what exactly do you mean? Well, in these days of players with modelling contracts and muscle tone, Lee still looks like one of us and we love him for it. I'm sure he spends hours down the gym. He just looks like he doesn't.

Are you trying to say he is an overweight alecart? Perish the thought, although Lee himself once said he started out as a short fat lad, progressed to being a tall skinny lad and ended up being a tall fat lad and I for one would never argue with Lee Crooks. Anyway I only said he *looked* like one of us. He's actually as good a player as any of those the young girls lust over. Lest we forget, Lee was once the most expensive player in the world and justifiably so.

Pardon? The Lee Crooks? Yes, although it may be hard for some of our younger readers to believe, Lee was once the most exciting forward in the game. Lee captained the Great Britain Colts on their first ever tour of Papua New Guinea and Australia in 1982, having already played the game since the age of eight. Later the same year he made his GB debut, making him then Great Britain's youngest ever forward. With his home town club of Hull he won every domestic honour (scoring eight out of 12 points in Hull's John Player Trophy victory over Hull KR in 1982) and was voted Young Player of the Year in 1985. So, when Leeds paid a then world record £150,000 for him, it seemed like a bargain.

A big name signing for Headingley? Let me guess, it didn't work out? His two-and-a-half years there are usually described as "unhappy" although he did well enough to be selected for his second tour of Australia in 1988 (his first was 1984). In 1990, he signed for Castleford for a then club record transfer fee and he's been the backbone of the team ever since.

What makes him so good? Lee is what's known as a "ball handling forward". This means he has skill to go alongside his brute strength always a useful package. He also specialises in impossible goal kicks. Connoisseurs of ridiculous angles well remember his last minute touchline penalty in the final test at Elland Road against New Zealand in 1985 which allowed Great Britain to draw the series.

Not to be confused with: Terry Crook, Thomas Cook's Tours, Lee Marvin, other big - boned players who make him look like Kate Moss.

Other big - boned players who make Lee Crooks look like Kate Moss? Frank Whitcombe, Brendan Hill, Paul Grayshon, Curiously all three played for Bradford Northern - although not all at the same time. The changing rooms wouldn't have been big enough.

Least likely to say: "Well, before the match I'm doing a fashion shoot for *Vogue*, then after it I'll be taking my shirt off for *Marie Claire*".

Most likely to say: "I'll get the beers in. What are you having?"

LEEDS 14
CAS 34

BITTER

"And I say the reindeer were offside!"

BOOZER'S LE PREMIER BIER

"What makes you think I forgot my keys and went to the pub after last nights match?"

Brian Bevan

Born: 24 June 1924. Died: 3 June 1991 (although when we last visited the Hall of Fame, they were claiming he was still alive).

Appearance: Bald, frail, toothless, bandy legged and covered in bandages.

What did he look like when he was young? That was if he ever was young. As far as we can tell Brian never looked particularly youthful.

The name's familiar. He had something to do with Warrington didn't he? Yes, he played for them between 1946 and 1962 and was probably the greatest winger who ever lived.

That's a bit of an extraordinary statement: He was a bit of an extraordinary player; one who scored a record 796 tries, over 200 more than his nearest rival (a Mr B. Boston of Wigan).

What made him so good? His speed and his side step. Comparisons with Martin Offiah could be made, especially as Brian reputedly wasn't much of a tackler either, but even Martin can't outfox defenders the way Bevan did. Some said he could run just as fast backwards as forwards!

But would he have got on A Question of Sport? Well he played Rugby Union at school so he would have stood a good chance.

Go on then, get out your Rothmans and give us some facts and figures: Okay then. He made 686 appearances, scored 2,456 points, twice touched down seven times in a single match and scored a hat-trick a staggering 69 times.

Any black spots in this catalogue of triumphs? Well to Warrington's eternal gratitude Leeds refused to give him a trial, and because he was based in Britain, he was never selected by the Kangaroos! Some would also point to the fact that he ended his career with Blackpool Borough (as indeed did Billy Boston).

Not to be confused with: John Bevan, Aneurin Bevan, Bev Bevan, Brian Blessed.

Do say: "Never has there been one to match the magic weaved by that awkward, elbowy emperor of our game."*

Don't say: "Isn't he that bald bloke who used to get slapped on the head by Benny Hill?"

* With permission from Grandstand Publications.
Page 19: The Official Rugby League Centenary Magazine- article by Colin Welland on Brian Bevan.

"What d' yu mean you've no PIES?!!"

The Flat Cappers   by Wilde

HARRY'S GAME

1994. BBC Look North Presenter Harry Gration tackles the RFL Public Relations job as David Howes moves on.

Maurice Lindsay

Description: The man who's going to drag Rugby League into the 21st century - whether it wants to go or not.

Ah Maurice Lindsay. What can you say about him that hasn't been said before? That he looks like Alec Gilroy off *Coronation Street*?

Well, apart from that, what can you say about Maurice that hasn't been said on the Rugby Leaguer's letters page many times already? Something complimentary? Maurice is a very controversial figure. I suspect even his friends divide into those who hate him and those who simply dislike him.

I read somewhere that he casts no shadow and sleeps in a coffin... or was that Count Dracula? For someone who calls himself the Prince of Darkness Count, Dracula is just a beginner compared to our Maurice. The Count only drank the blood of virgins. Maurice did something far worse. He tampered with the sacred traditions of Rugby League.

How could he? Has he no shame? Has he... Actually I couldn't care less about Rugby League's sacred traditions. Let's face it, doing something simply because it's always been done that way is the worse reason for doing anything. If we took tradition as holy writ we'd be still playing rugby union. Come to think of it, we'd still be playing with a round ball. So I say to hell with tradition! Steady on now you dangerous radical. You'll be saying that Rugby League works as a summer sport next... Actually it does work as a summer sport doesn't it? I enjoyed myself no end. It was really good to be able to go to Odsal and get a suntan rather than frost bite, and going to Paris was brilliant, and it was great to see London doing well and, hopefully, Wales will be great next year... and where were we?

We were giving Chairman Mo a satirical going over. Oh yes. Apparently he's a despotic autocrat who rules Rugby League with a rod of iron.

Good. There's plenty in the game who could do with some stick. All those whingers looking for someone to blame for the fact they couldn't run a bath without written instructions, never mind a rugby club. If they can't make Rugby League more attractive than a visit to a garden centre they deserve a damn good thrashing! You know, I'm starting to worry about you. Anyway Maurice picks fights with all the wrong people (fans, BARLA, the ARL) and has a startling ability to be able to open his mouth and put both his feet in it.

Well, it's a good trick if you can do it. I presume we're talking about his comment that in five years there would only be one code of rugby. I don't think I'd mind , as long of course as it has 13 players, no rucks, no mauls and a complete and total absence of line outs. I'm with you there. Anyway, Maurice later claimed he didn't make any such comment thus reinforcing many people's views that he's simply making it up as he goes along.

So Rugby League is still only a professional sport on the pitch. Off it it's still completely amateurish. Well at least that's one Rugby League tradition Maurice hasn't broken with. Yes, but that's the one we all wanted him to change.

Not to be confused with: Maurice Bamford, Maurice Oldroyd, Maurice Gibb, Darth Vader, Emperor Ming of Mongo, Tony Blair, Bet Lynch's former husband.

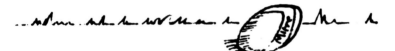

Phil Larder

Description: The modern coach *par excellence.*

So presumably he spends all his time on the touchline smoking tabs and shouting at his players? Can't you read? I said a *modern* coach. We're talking about the latest scientific coaching methods here; statistics, video analysis, training programmes, fitness levels, all that stuff. We're talking several hours a week spent analysing your opponent's game plan. We're talking even more time spent analysing your own team's performance and then preparing individual reports on each player. We are not talking motivating your players by shouting and swearing at them in - between gasps on your Woodbine.

No shouting, no swearing, no Woodbines. Are you sure this Larder bloke's a coach? He doesn't sound like one to me. Surely, at the very least he must rant and rave against the Australians? On the contrary, no - one's welcomed their influence more. The British game may have spent years learning the lessons of the 1982 tests but Phil started before the tests were even finished. The former school teacher and Oldham and Whitehaven player was so impressed by the Australians in the first test that, by the second, he was in their training camp studying their training methods. After that, he travelled to Australia itself and learnt directly from such coaching gurus as Frank Stanton, Ron Massey, Arthur Besteon and, most importantly, Jack Gibson.

So when it comes to coaching he wrote the book? He did and it's 320 pages long and forms the basis of British coaching at all levels. As Director of the National Coaching Scheme from 1982, Phil helped introduce such concepts as yardage and tackle counts to the British game and played a major part in closing the gap between Great Britain and Australia.

Ok so he knows his theory, but what about the practice? Can he cut it at club level? That's exactly what Phil wanted to know. So, in 1992, he signed up as coach with Widnes, and by the end of his first season had taken them to Wembley (caning Leeds 39-4 on the way there). Later he moved on to Keighley and with them won the Second Division Championship and Premiership double (although Keighley were denied any actual promotion because of Super League restructuring). In 1995, after serving as assistant GB coach to both Maurice Bamford and Mal Reilly, Larder became the England coach, reaching the World Cup final in 1995 and winning the European Championship in 1996. He's also the current coach of the full Great Britain side and by the time you read this he could be at a club near you (or not so near if he goes to Paris).

What? Surely Keighley aren't letting him go? The Cougars have decided not to renew his contract at the end of the 1996 season. Just why depends on who you believe. Keighley say it's because of poor results (The Cougars finished the 1996 season in second place missing out on promotion once again) while Larder says he was told that the club couldn't afford him (the Cougars are a First Division club but are reputedly paying Super League wages). Either way it's doubtful he'll be out of work too long.

Not to be confused with: Phil Lowe, Phil Ford, any number of coaches we're too nervous to name.

Least likely to say: "Bloody Australians. They're all right but they haven't got our natural ball skills".

BOZO FULTON'S CLASSIC WHINGES

33

"Buy a season ticket or I'll break yer nose!"

The Further Adventures of Mo   by Spencer

SHAUN & SHANE

For the first time that anyone can remember.... Wigan were dumped out of the 1996 Challenge Cup by Salford Reds!

Garry Schofield OBE

Description: Rugby League's Mr Nice Guy, cruelly deprived of the just rewards for his talents because of one simple mistake.

He forgot to wear gloves? No, he signed for Leeds.

I think we can kiss goodbye to any sales in the Headingley area. No, listen, the Loiners are cursed. Just look at the evidence. Garry's a great player. He's won 46 Great Britain international caps, tying with Mick Sullivan for the most ever. He's scored 31 international tries, second to the aforementioned Mr Sullivan, and made four tours down under. But what domestic honours has he got? Three Yorkshire Cup winners medals. And two of those he won with Hull.

I suppose it all started so well? It did. Garry captained Yorkshire and Great Britain schoolboys and the BARLA GB team before signing for Hull. He made his first team debut in September 1983 and was picked for the Great Britain under - 24 team just two months later. By the end of his first season he'd broken Hull's post - war try scoring record, become the youngest man ever to top the try scoring chart and been selected to tour Australia - again the youngest man ever. He'd also won exactly one third of his winners medals. He won his next the following season.

So when did he join Leeds? In October 1987 in a then record £155,000 deal. He quickly established himself as their top try scorer, and in October 1989 won his third winners medal when he scored two tries in Leeds' 33-12 defeat of Castleford. He won no more. Although Leeds got to several more finals in the next few years (including two consecutive Challenge Cup finals in, 94 and, 95) they didn't win any of them. Leeds were also runners-up for the Championship in 1989/90 and 1994/5. Close, but no big cigar. Eventually Schofield got bored waiting for Leeds to win something and went and joined Huddersfield.

Perhaps he should have left earlier? Many have wondered why he didn't. Garry's relationship with then Leeds coach Doug Laughton was, shall we say, notoriously strained, and didn't improve when chuggin' Doug signed the Great Britain and Wigan captain Ellery Hanley and gave him the captaincy that had previously been Garry's. Garry however got his revenge come the next Ashes tour taking the captaincy from the injured Hanley and never giving it back.

Was he a popular captain? Well the players liked him but the press liked him even more because, unlike his predecessor, he would actually talk to them. In fact he was so approachable he'd still be talking to them when the rest of the team were sitting at home watching TV.

Other victims of the Curse of Headingley: Too many to mention as we've only got a page but try Dean Bell and Yorkshire County Cricket Club.

Not to be confused with: Philip Schofield, Gary Connolly, Gary Glitter.

Most likely to say: "A quick interview? Ok".

Least likely to say: "**** off. I don't talk to journalists".

Schoey 46
Sully 46

Life Down South

In march 1993, Tony "The Tank" Gordon became London Crusaders coach. He soon had to learn about the second division, and in september, where the Crusaders' new stadium was.

"Tony was glad to be going first class next season!"

Tony The Tank Engine
by Dave Farrar

"Tony didn't know where Copthall was!"

Life Down South

"Tony was concerned about what Abi Ekoku would do to other teams' defences!"

Tony The Tank Engine
by Dave Farrar

"Tony was worried that he might be privatised!"

39

Dean Bell

Description: New Zealand's answer to the boomerang.

Pardon? You've lost me already. He's just like a boomerang, he always comes back. He first came to Britain in 1982 to play for Carlisle who agreed a payment of £1,000 after 20 matches. After the 20 matches had been played the club found they didn't actually have the money and eventually had to pay him in £200 instalments. Surprisingly, this experience didn't put him off the British game and, although he returned to Auckland at the end of the season, he came back the next to play for Leeds.

Now there's an experience to put him off the British game. Not on this occasion. Dean's arrival at Leeds coincided with that of Maurice Bamford as coach and that combination gave Leeds a run of 18 matches without defeat and cup final success in the John Player Trophy. Dean then left to play for Australia's Eastern Suburbs for a couple of seasons but when he came back it was to join Wigan.

Let me guess. Cup, trophy, trophy, cup. Cup, cup, cup. Trophy, trophy. I'm afraid so. In his first season as captain Wigan won its first treble of League, Premiership and Challenge Cup, as well as the Charity Shield, the World Club Challenge and the Sydney Sevens. Dean himself won the Man of Steel award in 1992 and even appeared on *This Is Your Life*. Along the way he also picked up 26 test caps for New Zealand and played in the 1988 World Cup final against Australia.

Then I presume he went down under again? Yes, back to New Zealand to join his former Wigan coach John Monie at the newly formed Auckland Warriors. In March 1995 Dean led them out for their first ever match, one which was watched on over 70% of the TV sets in New Zealand. However Dean just can't keep away and he returned to Great Britain later the same year to become assistant coach at Leeds.

The latest instalment in a brilliant career? It should have been. Leeds were one of Britain's biggest clubs and it should have been the ideal place to learn the coaching ropes. However, no sooner had Dean got off the plane than chief coach Doug Laughton had resigned, throwing Dean in at the deep end. He started well: Leeds came second in the Centenary Season (although it could have been claimed that no one else was really trying too hard), but then all the big names began to leave and Dean wasn't given the money to replace them. Results started going against them and only the presence of Paris and Workington prevented Leeds from being real candidates for relegation.

So presumably Dean will soon be going down under again, this time to sign on. Actually no - one really blames Dean. He was just unfortunate enough to be in charge when the money ran out. Besides things may not be as bad as they seem. Leeds have lots of talented youngsters (both its Alliance and Academy teams did well) and if they only can hang on to them, the future should be brighter. Let's hope so. Rugby League needs a strong Leeds. If only because it makes beating them so much more enjoyable.

Not to be confused with: his uncle Cameron Bell (coached Carlisle), his brother Ian Bell (also played for Carlisle) his cousin Clayton Friend (also played for Carlisle), Alexander Graham Bell (invented the telephone, never played for Carlisle).

Least likely to say: "I'm really glad I came back to Headingley, Alf."

Most likely to say: "Could I have a return ticket to Auckland please?"

LOINERS

WIGAN

Spencer 95

41

Life Down South

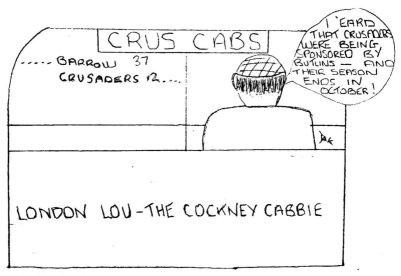

A Typical London Rugby League Supporter

Tony The Tank Engine
by Dave Farrar

"Tony was concerned that the scoreboard man might be overworked!"

Life Down South

Les Miserable
The Saddest Man South Of Doncaster

In 1994, the Crusaders became the London Broncos.
Some fans were never going to be happy...

Frano Botica

Description: Robotica the Kiwi Points Machine.

Oh yes I know the one. Never misses. Every time someone scores a try, he slots the conversion over the uprights. It's all a bit dull actually. It'd be a lot more exciting if he missed occasionally. Most clubs would kill to be so bored. If you're in the habit of playing tight matches, a dependable kicker can make all the difference and, since signing from the All Blacks in 1990, none have been more dependable than Frano.

Go on then dazzle us with some facts and figures. I know you're dying to. Anything to oblige. Frano scored his 1000 points in only 93 games, a Rugby League record. He was the League's leading goal kicker and points scorer in 1991/92 (161 goals, 364 points), 1993/4 (188 goals, 422 points) and 1994/95 (186 goals, 408 points). In the year he failed to reach the top (1992/3) he still scored 423 points but was beaten by Keighley Cougars' John Wasyliw who scored a staggering 490 points - the third highest of all time.

Of course you can only score all those points if someone else scores a lot of tries for you to convert. True, and Frano was fortunate to play for Wigan when Offiah, Edwards and company were at their most prolific. That's why the points have slowed down since joining Castleford in November 1995. They just don't score as many tries.

Let's face it though, his kicking should be good. He's a former Union player, they do more kicking than the Cancan girls at the Folies-Bergere. Thankfully there's more to Frano than what he does with his boot. He's a good all-rounder, one of the best stand-offs in the game as he showed in the inaugural Super League season when Castleford beat Bradford - or as one disillusioned Cas fan put it: when the Bulls were defeated by "Botica and 12 puddings" (and we've cleaned that one up a bit!)

The All Blacks. Are they any good? Well, for a Union team they're not bad at all and many observers put this down to the fact that they're actually playing Rugby League with two extra men. Indeed, a lot of their players such as Jonah Lomu (the big bloke in the pizza ad) are former League players. Since being an All Black is a lucrative occupation, few of them make the jump to League but those who do don't do too badly. Take for example Va'aiga Tuigamala or Craig Innes...

What about John Gallagher? Even he wasn't as bad as everyone remembers - just not as good as we were all led to expect.

Not to be confused with: Frank Bough, Franco Nero, Carter the Unstoppable Sex Machine.

Most likely to say: "Oh well, there's another two for the board."

Least likely to say: "You take this one. I'm feeling a little rusty."

"But Ref... You let them get away with scoring from a forward pass!"

The Flat Cappers

by Wilde

SHIRT TALES

Eddie Waring MBE

Description: Rugby League's most controversial figure; an embarrassment to some, an icon to others.

Surely you're exaggerating? He was only a TV commentator after all: Yes, but probably the most famous TV commentator of all time. In the 1970s an 'Eddie Waring' was compulsory for all aspiring impressionists and Eddie Waring Appreciation Societies sprang up all over the country. The man himself broke out of the sports ghetto to appear with both the *Goodies* and *Morecambe* and *Wise*.

Sounds good. So where's the problem? Although much-loved outside the game, Eddie's distinctive style had his critics within it whose views were summed up by Reg Bowden when he said that Eddie had "done as much for the image of our sport as Cyril Smith would do for hang-gliding". 10,000 people once signed a petition asking for him to be removed because his commentaries were "an insult which turned the game into a music hall joke".

So Eddie's persona non grata in RL circles then? Sadly, Eddie is no longer with us but his reputation is now on the up.

Why's that? Some of it's just seventies nostalgia. To younger fans Eddie was much a part of their childhood as Spangles, John Noakes and Chopper bikes. However, it goes deeper than that. Although his new fans acknowledge that perhaps he carried on too long (he did his first commentary in 1951 and didn't retire until 1981) and could lapse into self-parody (especially on *It's a Knockout*), they appreciate his genuine achievements.

What, being mandatory for contestants on New Faces? There was far more to Eddie than that. He was a visionary manager of Dewsbury in the 1940s, stealing ideas from American football decades before the Australians did it and winning the wartime Challenge Cup and two Championships for his trouble. He then became a journalist for the *Sunday Pictorial* and later the *Sunday Mirror*, paying his own passage to Australia to cover the 1946 Lions tour. His book *The Great Ones* is very well regarded by those lucky enough to have a copy.

Yes, but what about his TV work? Well Eddie was capable of a lyricism far beyond his successors. His "poor lad" is Rugby League's equivalent of "they think it's all over" and in a fairer world would just be as famous. Besides which he was a nationally recognised figure, as famous in Catford as Castleford and how many of those has Rugby League had?

Not to be confused with: Eddie Butler, Fred Waring and his Pennsylvanians, Ray French.

Most likely to say: "And 'es going for an early bath."

Least likely to say: "The atmosphere must be white hot down there Alex", "Yes and it's very warm too Ray"

Also unlikely to say: "And why did he kick?... oh, and he's scored."

A RIGHT UP 'N UNDER

IT'S A KNOCK OUT

49

ON THE ROAD TO OZ

WIGAN'S PHIL CLARKE AND DENIS BETTS MUST HAVE HAD A PREMONITION OF HOW POINTLESS AND BORING THE CENTENARY SEASON WAS WHEN THEY HEADED OFF DOWN UNDER AT THE END OF THE 1994-95 SEASON! CLARKE SIGNED A THREE YEAR DEAL WITH SYDNEY-BASED EASTERN SUBURBS ROOSTERS, WHILE BETTS JOINED THE AUCKLAND WARRIORS.

TO THE WINFIELD CUP

51

Kelvin Skerrett

Description: Mad, bad and dangerous to know. Allegedly.

Kelvin does have something of a reputation doesn't he? Oh yes. He's the type of player who's always referred to by journalists as "rugged".

You sound sceptical. You're not claiming Kelvin Skerrett is innocent are you? Well not so much innocent. No – one who saw the infamous "Flying Skerretts" incident could ever claim that. Just not always guilty or at least no more guilty than many others.

Are you saying Kelvin has a reputation he can't live up to? Well at the 1995 World Cup, the Dance Theatre of Fiji's mock battle, with its display of swinging punches, kung fu kicks and swan dives was universally greeted with a cry of "it's Kelvin Skerrett" but he wasn't sent off at all that season. In fact, Neil Cowie was the only pie eater to be sent off the entire season, which compares more than favourably to St Helen's seven early baths. Admittedly, Kelvin seems to spend half his time injured these days which cuts down his opportunities for mayhem but then could even a fit Kelv compete with Matt Calland of Featherstone and now Bradford who's been sent off five times in the last two seasons? Indeed the Bulls have frequently been unable to finish a match with the same number of players they started with. This might have been a problem if it wasn't for the fact that they play better with only 12 men.

Still, at least Kelvin has more than just a bad name. He has a few winner's medals as well. Well he has been playing for Wigan since 1990 so understandably he's picked up a few. He's also more than a dozen Great Britain caps and in the last few years has been collecting Welsh ones too.

Is Kelvin Welsh? He never sounds like he comes from the land of song where men are men and sheep are worried! Unless of course the song is on Ilkley Moor Baht 'at. Kelvin may sound like an *Emmerdale* cast member but let's face it if he thinks he's Welsh are you going to be the person who tells him he isn't? Actually, although Kelvin comes from Leeds he qualifies as Welsh because he has a Welsh granny. His Wigan colleagues Neil Cowie and Martin Hall are also born again Welshmen, while his uncle Trevor Skerrett also played for Wales back in the late seventies.

If Kelvin's a Leeds lad, presumably he played for Leeds? Don't be daft. Until recently Leeds lads never played for Leeds. Like Kelvin they started with Hunslet and then moved on to clubs outside the city, in Kelvin's case Bradford Northern. (Other products of the Hunslet talent school include Sonny Nickle). Leeds lads only ever play for Leeds when they come back as big – name signings (for example Messrs Schofield and Hanley). This is, of course, something Kelvin may well do if, as expected, he leaves Central Park at the end of the 1996 season. Unless, of course, he returns to Bradford...

Not to be confused with: Melvin Bragg, the Kelvin scale of temperature, Harry Secombe, Kevin Kline.

Most likely to say: "But ref, I never touched him".

WALES 22
W. SAMOA 10

SPENCER 95

The Further Adventures of Mo   by Spencer

MAL, CLIFF & SHAUN

The 1994 Great Britain v Australia Ashes Series kicked off with Cliff Richard doing the pre-match entertainment.

Mal Meninga

Description: Great Britain's favourite Australian.

Why's that? Did he gift us that try that finally allowed us to win back the Ashes? Some chance. Over the last 15 years Mal played a major part in depriving us of victory, scoring more points against us than any other Australian player.

And we still like him? Well the British have always been suckers for a mixture of talent and charisma.

Good was he? Well, back in Australia he made 11 Grand Final appearances (five for Canberra, six for Brisbane/Souths) and played for Queensland 41 times (including a record 32 State of Origin matches). Internationally he has more caps than any other Australian, and was the first player ever to take part in four Ashes tours (1982, 86, 90 and 94), and the first to captain Australia on two. He also helped Australia to win the World Cup in 1992 and, when he wasn't thrashing Britain, he led Australia to victory in test series against France, New Zealand and Papua New Guinea.

Winners medals don't make people love you though do they? What's his secret? Mal played with a combination of strength, grace, resilience and bravery in the face of an appalling injury. He broke his arm in May 1987 and in the next 18 months, while making comebacks, broke it another three more times. That he didn't give up there and then but came back to lead his country is both a tribute to his courage and an inspiration to other injured players.

Is Mal as popular down under as he is here? Let's just say we spotted his greatness early. For a long time Mal had his critics in Australia who thought he was lazy, a natural athlete who didn't push himself enough. He proved them all wrong. Now, by and large, Australia agrees with us. Mal was one of the greats.

Most likely to love him: St Helens fans (Mal played for them in 1984/85, scoring 28 tries in 31 games and revitalising the club); the BBC (who made him Overseas Sports Personality of the year and got him on *A Question of Sport*).

Least likely to love him: London Broncos fans (Mal was rumoured to be joining them for a season but retired instead); the racist spectator he once thumped at the end of a game; the ARL after he signed up as a figurehead for Super League.

Not to be confused with: Mal Reilly, Mel Gibson, Bobby Fulton (Great Britain's least favourite Australian).

Life Down South

Broncos' supporters were still hoping for superstars

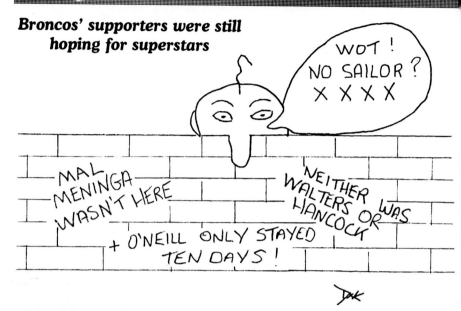

by Dave Farrar

The Broncos' tactics were sometimes questioned

Q-"I Say, I Say, I Say. Why are the Broncos like the Dodo?"
A-"Because neither of them could use their wings!"

Life Down South

Superstars were promised...

by Dave Farrar

But other clubs' concerns about the number of Australians were confirmed...

Jonathan Davies MBE

Description: Rugby union player turned Rugby League player turned rugby union player.

Hang on, you can't do that! You can now. Since union started openly paying its players last year its' excuse for discriminating against Rugby League has disappeared and some players have returned to it, Jonathan Davies unsurprisingly being one of the first.

Unsurprisingly? Jonathan never made a secret of his desire to return to Welsh rugby union in some capacity or other. (That's why he never criticised it and always denied the existence of boot money - he didn't want to blot his copy book too much). Therefore, the opportunity to return as a player was just too good to miss. After all, at 32 his Rugby League career was almost over but in union he could play on for years. He could even revive his international career.

Was he worth the £250,000 Widnes were reputed to have offered him to switch to League? It seemed doubtful at the time but Jonathan adapted to League far better than many expected. By the end of his second season he'd scored a club record 342 points and picked up medals for the First Division Championship, Charity Shield and Lancashire Cup. He quickly made the Great Britain team and scored in all five tests against Papua New Guinea and New Zealand in 1990. He captained Great Britain against France in 1992 and even the most sceptical of doubters were won over by his try in Great Britain's 12 – man victory against Australia in 1994. He also played a major part in the revived Welsh Rugby League team which won the European Championship in 1995 and reached the World Cup semi-finals the same year. He won the award for First Division Player of the Year in 1991 and both that award and the Man of Steel in 1994. By this time, of course, he was a Warrington player.

I bet he cost the Wire a penny or two. Actually he didn't cost them anything at all, at least not in transfer fees. Widnes were so hard up by then they were willing to let him go for free to any team willing to pick up his expensive contract. (He'd almost gone to Wakefield earlier in the season but they backed out worried about the effect the size of his wage packet would have on their other players). Then to add to his riches Jonathan made a killing in the Super League wars when signing up with the ARL for a reported £2,000,000.

So why isn't he in Australia? Small print. His contract with the ARL didn't actually commit him to play for them, just not to play for Super League. Therefore, by returning to rugby union he was able to get out of it and keep the money (and Warrington were able to get a £60,000 transfer fee, whereas had he gone to an ARL club they wouldn't have got anything).

So has Rugby League seen the last of Jonathan Davies? Rumours that he will be involved with the new South Wales Super League club in some capacity have so far proved untrue so, at the moment, Davies-spotters can still find him at union matches with a bored expression on his face waiting for someone to pass him the ball.

Least likely to say: "Rugby union is rubbish. I can't believe I spent so long playing it."

Most likely to say: "Could you make it payable to Mr J. Davies please."

Life Down South

Les Miserable
The Saddest Man South Of Doncaster

Life Down South

BRONCOS SIGN "THE FRIDGE"

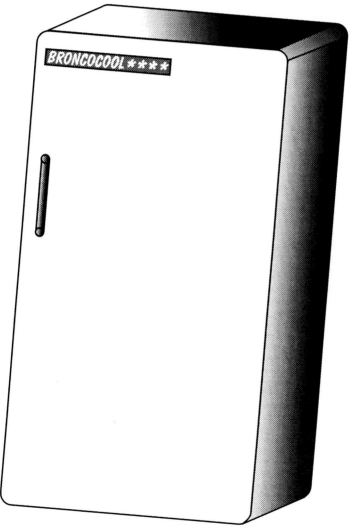

BRONCOCOOL ✱✱✱

...BUT ONLY TO KEEP THE FOSTER'S IN!!!

Karl Harrison

Born: 20 February 1964.

Appearance: Big and brawny.

He's big but is he any good? There is a Rugby League saying that "A good big 'un will always beat a good little 'un". Well they don't come much bigger or better than Halifax Blue Sox's Karl Harrison.

Yeah, but what has he done?: A Great Britain and England regular since 1990, he has been the cornerstone of his country's pack with that other Yorkshireman Kelvin Skerrett, as a serious rival.

Any other claim to fame? He has twice been on the winning side against mighty Australia at Wembley in 1990 and 1994. Alas, he couldn't make it a hat - trick in the 1995 World Cup Final at the grand old Empire Stadium.

Where did you say he was from? Karl is as Yorkshire as Yorkshire pudding and Yorkshire curd tart. His list of clubs reads like a tour of the county of the broad acres: Bramley, Featherstone, Hull and the Halifax Blue Sox. Quite what Karl would have said a few years ago if someone had suggested that he would become one of the original Blue Sox is hard to imagine.

But is he going anywhere? Not likely, Leeds couldn't afford him! Karl, now in his thirties, looks set to finish his career at Thrum Hall and he remains the hardest of props in the old tradition who can blast the toughest of defences and put the fear of God into opponents.

Not to be confused with: Harrison Ford, Iestyn Harris, Harris Tweed, Boris Karloff.

Don't say: 'Didn't you used to play for Lancashire?'

FAX 27
CHEMICS 10

"Like I said at the outset... Mergers are not on the agenda!"

The Flat Cappers   # by Wilde

Panel 1: They reckon a local lad's won t'lottery. He's given his winnins to t'club. — Oh Aye?

Panel 2: Aye, reckons e's gunna fix t'bogs, mend t'roof and buy some new players.

Panel 3: Just think on worr' e cud've done if e'd've come up wi' FOUR balls!!

WELCOME TO SCUT LA HOME OF SCUTTERTON SCORPIONS

Deryck Fox

Description: Featherstone's adopted son.

Are we talking loyalty, not loyalty bonus here? Like acne and pogo sticks, loyalty bonuses are only for the young and Deryck's pretty elderly now. Well over 30 anyway. Besides which he's never been the sort to fly off to Australia for a couple of fivers. Apart from a relatively brief spell with Bradford Northern he's spent his professional career with Featherstone Rovers, who aren't known for their free spending ways. He joined them from Dewsbury amateurs St John Fisher back in 1983 and stayed there for the next nine years. When he did finally leave it was to follow the club coach Peter Fox over to Bradford, and when Peter left them Deryck returned to Featherstone.

So he's into family loyalty as well as club loyalty? Deryck isn't actually part of the famous Fox family, although his dad and Peter did both play for Batley. His departure from the rechristened Bulls owed less to either devotion to the older Mr Fox or dislike of the new name and more to the fact that they only wanted players willing to go full time. Deryck, a fork – lift truck driver during working hours, thought he was a bit old to make that jump.

Call me cynical, but is he any good? It's easy to be loyal to your club if no – one else wants you. Well Deryck has managed to win more than a dozen international caps over the years. He made a two – try debut against France in 1985 and later that year played in all three tests against New Zealand. He played in two tests against Australia in 1986 and was a stalwart of the mid - week touring team in 1992. He also scored all Great Britain's points in their World Cup final defeat against Australia. All this despite playing for unglamorous clubs in one of the positions Great Britain were strongest in. Poor old Deryck had to compete with Andy Gregory, Shaun Edwards and Bobbie Goulding for his team place.

It's just occurred to me that given that no one in Featherstone had a good word for Super League, they've done pretty well out of it haven't they? Well I thought they had several good words for Super League, although admittedly you wouldn't be able to use any of them on children's television. But to answer your question, yes they have. Not only have they got their share of the cash (which unlike that given to Super League clubs has no strings attached to what it is spent on), they've assembled a strong team of players like Deryck, Roy Powell and Neil Summers who've had to drop down a division because they couldn't become full time professionals.

Great ill – timed injuries of our time: Deryck once injured himself while kicking off in the Regal Trophy final. The only more unfortunate injury we know of belonged to Dean Bell who once strained a leg while warming up for the World Club Challenge.

Not to be confused with: Peter Fox (wears a baseball cap, shouts a bit), Neil Fox (scored a lot of points apparently), Don Fox (a poor lad, the Nathan Graham of his generation), Fox's Biscuits (sponsors of Batley RLFC).

Definitely not to be confused with: Posh – voiced actor Edward Fox (famous for his portrayals of the Duke of Windsor in *Edward & Roger Simpson* and baby – faced assassin Brendan Tuuta in (*The Day of the Tackle*); Sam Fox (no missus, those aren't two rugby balls shoved up her jumper), Basil Brush.

Life Down South

Maranta & Son
by Dave Farrar

Life Down South

BRONCO CURRIE HOUSE AND TAKEAWAY

Koalas and possums our speciality

HOT AND TASTY!
BUT CAN CURRIE DELIVER?

Ellery Hanley MBE

Also known as: The black pearl, the greatest living Yorkshireman, "salary" Hanley.

Description: The finest player of his generation and the proof positive of the redemptive powers of Rugby League.

Are we talking about a full trophy cabinet? To put it mildly. Three Man of Steel awards (1985, 87, 89), an Adidas Golden Boot (1989), the Lance Todd Trophy (1989) and 35 international caps which he won by playing in four different positions (making him the third most capped player ever). Plus the normal number of winners medals you'd expect for a player who captained the almighty Wigan from the mid 80's to the early 90's. He also topped the try scoring tables in 1985 and 1987.

I'm beginning to be impressed. Oh, we've hardly started yet. In 1988 Ellery won a place in sporting history when he became the first black captain of a British team (in any sport) and then won a place in sporting hearts by leading the team to victory in the historic Third Test. Britain's first victory against the Australians since 1978. In 1994 Ellery made history again when he became the first ever black coach of a British national team, again in any sport.

Ok. I'm impressed. So you should be. Even the Australians were after he led Balmain to their first Grand Final in 19 years in 1988.

Popular with the press was he? Not really. After one of the tabloids had a bit too much digging in his "humble background" he refused to speak to them, any of them, for a decade. Even when he was GB captain.

That must have made the post match press conferences interesting. Well he did actually talk to the media on a couple of occasions. He once appeared on Channel 4's *Jonathan Ross Show* to plug the London Monarchs.

What the American football team? Yes, years before The Fridge Ellery was their first big name signing. They paid him a shed full of money but he never actually played a game for them.

And the other time he broke his silence? He took a job as a commentator for Australian TV. Ironically enough he was then sacked because no one could understand his accent.

Not to be confused with: Jenny Hanley, Tommy Handley, Ellery Queen.

Most likely to say: Nothing.

Least likely to say: Anything at all.

GT BRITAIN 5
AUSTRALIA 4

Spencer '94

73

It didn't matter what rule changes they introduced....
No one was going to rip our Gary's balls out!!

The Further Adventures of Mo   by Spencer

KICK OFF

BOOZER'S BEST BITTER

HALF TIME

BOOZER'S BEST BITTER

YOUR UNCLE ARNOLD'S WHIPPET'S SHOWN NO SIGN OF EXCITEMENT ALL MATCH!

FULL TIME

THAT'S COZ IT'S STUFFED.... YOU DROP KICK!

BOOZER'S BEST BITTER

A BIT LIKE YOUR TEAM THEN!!

BOOZER'S BEST BITTER

Spencer 96—

Martin Offiah

He's Irish isn't he? Chariots O'Fire. It's actually pronounced Off-iah. It's Nigerian.

Chariots Off-iah. It doesn't make sense: The nick name "Chariots" is just a figment of a PR man's imagination (presumably the same one who mispronounced his surname). His friends call him 'Tin' (as in Mar-tin).

PR men don't usually pay much attention to RL players. Why the interest here? Well, since signing for Widnes from Rosslyn Park RUFC in 1987 he's made such an impression on Rugby League that even people outside the sport have noticed him. Basically he scores tries, lots of them and in great style. In his debut season he won the Man of Steel award by topping the try scoring table with 44. He topped it again the following year with 60, and the next year with 45 and so on. He's now scored well over 400 tries which puts him among the top 10 try scorers of all time.

He can't tackle though, can he? He's not there to tackle. There's 12 other players to do that. Martin's job is to race down the wing leaving defenders trailing hopelessly in his wake. And when you can do that 10 times in a single match (as he did against Leeds in 1992) you've earned your money.

He's not what he was though, is he? Martin is said to have lost "a yard of pace" by those who say that sort of thing and when he scores these days it tends to be from a shorter distance. However he still topped the try scoring tables in 1994/95 and 1995/96, and London Broncos (and Bedford RUFC) wouldn't have paid £300,000 for a player who was past it. Even if he was though, the TV people would probably still love him.

Oh yes, I thought I'd seen him on TV? Seen him? he's never off it! Martin is easily television's favourite RL player. *Question of Sport, Gladiators, Sports Personality of the Year, Emmerdale,* that one with Eamonn Holmes; he does them all. When *They Think It's All Over* get around to having a Rugby League player in to insult, you can guarantee that player will be Martin.

Why do TV producers love him so much? Well, it would be nice if we could put it all down to an appreciation of his talents, but let's face it, if he was pug ugly we wouldn't see half as much of him. Martin is very photogenic.

And? I feel you're holding back? Well some suspect Martin is popular with TV types because, unlike other League players, he doesn't sound Northern. In fact, due to his background (his mother's a school teacher, his father a Nigerian magistrate) and his education (he went to Wolverstone Hall boarding school) he sounds distinctly posh.

He doesn't sound that posh: He does compared to Lee Crooks.

Most likely to say: "Ian will kill me if I'm wrong David, but I reckon it's Damon Hill."

Least likely to say: "E were a great baker, were our dad."

Life Down South

by Dave Farrar

London on Tour!

Life Down South

Bronco in Paris

Bronco panicked when he heard they could eat him!

Les Miserable
The Saddest Man South Of Doncaster

Eddie & Stevo

Description: Sky TV's answer to Cannon and Ball.

So are they a pair of comedians then? Well, that's a matter of opinion. They're actually Sky's Super League commentary team. Eddie Hemmings is an urbane frontman of the Elton Welsby/Steve Ryder school (not quite Des Lynam), while Mike "Stevo" Stephenson is an opinionated summariser in the Alex Murphy mould. In fact, Stevo could be described as the Anti-Murphy.

Er... How come... ? The two of them are so alike and yet, in one vital respect, so different. Both are distinguished former players (Stevo was with Dewsbury when they won the 1973 championship and scored against Australia in Britain's 1972 World Cup victory). Both became coaches (Stevo with the Australian club Penrith). Both now vigorously air their strongly held views on the airwaves and in the newspapers. It's just that these views differ widely. Take any subject: summer rugby, squad numbers, mergers and they'll probably disagree on it. Alex is a traditionalist, Stevo is a moderniser and I wouldn't like to be trapped in a lift with the pair of them.

What about Eddie then? Eddie is a former football commentator who apparently wasn't into Rugby League before he got the job but who now can't get enough. Eddie thinks everything is "great" ("That was a great try from a great player. This is turning into a great match").

Enough about the boys, what about the coverage? Is it any good? It's fair to say that Sky have revolutionised the way Rugby League is presented in this country (more cameras, replays from different angles, etc). They've also allowed championship matches to be seen for the first time by the whole country - or at least those parts of it with satellite dishes. Previously, if these matches were shown at all it was only on regional TV, and then not until sometime after *Cell Block H*. The BBC has only ever shown cup matches: either pre-existing ones like the Challenge Cup and the fixture-clogging Regal Trophy, or specially created ones like the Floodlit Trophy.

There's all that hype though isn't there and the way they keep going on about how "great" Super League is. Well they've spent £87 million on it so they're hardly going to tell you it's awful. More annoying is the way Sky ignores the First and Second Divisions (but then they could argue so do most of the fans) and the way that Rugby League's first and only magazine programme *Boots 'n' All* has turned into a ragbag of last week's highlights shuttling round Sky schedules like a ball bearing in a pinball machine. Still, it may not be perfect but it's better than the alternatives. For a start, you'll never find Stevo referring to that "great Dewsbury side of the seventies."

Not to be confused with: Morecambe and Wise, Little and Large, Pearl and Dean, PJ and Duncan.

Most likely to say: "This is what Super League is all about. Great games, great players, great balls of fire."

Least likely to say: "And we'll have the second half of the match after the 3.30 from Kempton Park and don't forget next week we have some real rugby from Murrayfield."

"Hello Coach. Scott's too ill to train... That's right...
He's as sick as a dog!"

"Sorry about the delay ref... We'll kick off as soon as the
lads find the ball!"

Alex Murphy

Also known as: Murphy the Mouth.

Description: Columnist, commentator, greyhound enthusiast, player, coach and Rugby League legend.

What makes him so special? Great players frequently make mediocre players and average coaches but it's rare for a great player to become a great coach.

Alex is that rarity? Indeed he is. A teenage signing for St Helens, Alex scored a hat-trick on his senior debut and went on to score 275 in 575 matches. Along the way he appeared in 19 major finals and became the first man to captain three different teams to victory at Wembley (St Helens in 1961 and 1966, Leigh in 1971 and Warrington in 1974). The last two times were as coach with Leigh and Warrington, he also coached Wigan, St Helens and Huddersfield and Alex won 16 trophies and came close to capturing several more (we won't talk about his strangely barren stay at Salford). His test debut at 19 made him Great Britain's youngest ever tourist and he went on to get another 26 caps. He later coached England in the 1975 International Championship, failing to win it by a single point.

What's the secret of his success? As both player and coach, Alex doesn't know the meaning of the word failure. He's also a bit hazy on the meanings of the words modesty and self-restraint.

Some Murphy legends please. Alex was whisked away after an amateur match on the eve of his 16th birthday and signed for St Helens at the stroke of midnight. His international career was cut short, not by injury or lack of form, but because he refused to tour if he wasn't made captain. He once told Aussie TV that he wouldn't trust a top opposition coach to train his greyhounds. He left Wigan after throwing a telephone at Maurice Lindsay. After his departure from Huddersfield he used the club's phone-in club call to denounce the directors who sacked him. At Leigh the club paid his phone bill, and once his electricity bill as well after he told them: "what do you expect me to do, phone in the dark?"

So what is he doing now? *Enjoying a quiet retirement?* Some chance of that, he's back at Warrington, this time as Director of Football, but even if he was in retirement it wouldn't be quiet. Alex is one of the most quotable men in RL and if he likes the sound of his own voice, journalists like it even more. Alex is always good copy: Aussie coaches, squad numbering, summer rugby, modern coaching methods; you name it, Alex can sound off about it.

Not to be confused with: Peter Fox, Maurice Bamford, Brian Clough.

Least likely to say: "I think renaming the club Blue Sox is a good idea."

Most likely to be found: "In the changing rooms taking the paint off the walls with his half-time team talk."

NEWCKY BRUWN

The Flat Cappers   by Wilde

TARQUIN THE SCOREBOARD

HARLEQUINS	TRIES 0
VISITORS	TRIES 0

Hello! My name is Tarquin. I'm the scoreboard at The Stoop, home of Harlequins RUFC in Twickenham. Mine is a lonely job. I mean, how would you like to be stuck up one end of the ground, exposed to all the elements and forced to watch rugby union? It's not as if anything exciting ever happens! From what I can see, and I'm no expert 'cos I'm only a scoreboard, they get the ball and instead of passing it as I thought you are meant to do, they kick the damn thing into touch.

The ball is out of play so often, the players get no chance of scoring a try. No I tell a lie. The other day a miracle happened, this Harlequins geezer did score a try, but my parts had seized up through lack of use and I was stuck at no score. Luckily one of them had a tin of 3-in-1 which lubricated my vital parts [phnahh, phnahh], and I was able to register the correct score.

This contrasts nicely with a visit from you League boys the other day. Who were you playing? St Hallibuts or someone? Anyway all I can say is I've never worked so hard in my life! Only a couple of minutes had gone and you Broncos chappies had already scored two tries. I hadn't even had a chance to sip my glass of creosote. In fact I was so excited by the game that I got all of a fluster and started to show 5 points for a try. Then St Hillbillies scored and scored and scored! I was pleased when half time arrived. I was in need of a good rest! I counted 15 tries in that game. About as many as Harlequins and their opponents have scored in four dull matches here.

Anyway, thanks for the chance to do some work for a change. Don't suppose you've got any vacancies for a scoreboard have you?

Tarquin the Scoreboard.

by Lol Ferrier

Iestyn Harris

Description: Youthful Welsh wizard (sort of...)

Lechyd da! Pardon?

Lechyd da! Good health! He's a boy from the Vallies isn't he? Only if you mean those to be found between the hills of Oldham.

You mean he's not Welsh? With a name like that I thought he must have be one of League's union signings. Iestyn was born and raised in Oldham. He's a product of the amateur RL club Oldham St Annes and has never played union, (well at least not so far). However, his parents *are* Welsh and that's how he qualifies to play in the Welsh Rugby League team with whom he won International Player of the Year in 1995.

Ah, so young, so talented... so expensive. Iestyn's currently on the transfer market for a staggering £1.35 million. That's roughly three Martin Offiahs (at 1992 prices).

£1.35 million? You could buy an entire team for that. Or indeed an entire club; lock, stock and oak – panelled board room. Initially it was thought that Warrington were simply trying to price him out of the market but relations between Iestyn and the Wire's management team of Alex Murphy and John Dorahy are now so bad that it must be assumed that it's for real.

Good grief, fancy falling out with Alex Murphy and John Dorahy. It's unheard of. After all, they're such easy going, mild mannered chaps. What's at the root of all this trouble? Well if it's not money (and Iestyn claims it's not) everyone assumes it's how he spends the off season. Some of Iestyn's former Welsh team-mates now spend their winters playing rugby union and they're suspected of persuading him to come and join them. However, Alex Murphy has said that his players are Rugby League players and can forget about playing anything else. Therefore, if Iestyn wants to try his hand at kick – and – chase he'll have to go elsewhere.

So where's he going to end up? The price is out of reach of most League clubs, especially since perennial big spenders Leeds and Wigan are both short of the readies at the moment. However, it has been suggested that the new South Wales club may win his signature, sharing him and the transfer fee with a Union club. Then again, given that there seems to be a surfeit of millionaires with more money than taste, a union club may well sign him outright which would be a tragedy almost as much for him as for the game.

Not to be confused with: Richard Harris, "Bomber" Harris, Keith Harris and Orville.

Most likely to say: "Jonathan was wrong. This game is rubbish."

Least likely to say: "Ydych chi'n siarad Cymraeg?"

The Further Adventures of Mo   by Spencer

OH! OH! SEVENS

11th May 1996. Wigan become first Rugby League team to play at Twickenham and win Middlesex Sevens Championship

Robbie Paul

Description: Rugby League's next superstar

Talented is he? And then some. Already much loved by the Bradford fans, Robbie burst into into national prominence at the 1996 Challenge Cup Final when at 20 he became the youngest ever Wembley captain. He then went on to prove just why he was made captain by scoring the first ever hat-trick in a Challenge Cup Final. He also won the Lance Todd Trophy - despite being on the losing side.

Young and talented. I hate him already: You'll hate him even more when I tell you he is an artist off the pitch as well as on it. He was at art school when he signed for Bradford and still paints in oils in his spare time. He also makes sculptures out of beef bones (don't ask), and found the time to provide Bradford's "Run With The Bulls" rap record.

So he's Alex Murphy, Picasso and Ice T rolled into one then? Any more like him at home? Brother Henry has already made a name for himself over at Wigan. He's a handy player as well, and modest with it too. He spent several years telling disbelieving journos that his little brother was the talented one in the family.

Hopefully we'll see them playing for England: Sadly not. They're from New Zealand, the latest in a long line of great Kiwi players to grace the British game which includes Dean Bell, Graeme West, Kurt Sorensen, Dave Watson (when off the demon weed), Frano Botica, Kevin Tamati, all the Ropatis, Hull KR's double - winning trio Gary Prohm, Mark Broadhurst and Gordon Smith, and others too numerous to mention.

Why are there so many Kiwis playing in Britain? British bargain hunters have long realised that for the price of an average Aussie you can get a great Kiwi. Kiwis also tend to stick around longer (for a career rather than for a season), and even if they do go away they tend to come back again (e.g. Mr Bell and Mr Botica).

Why is that? Aussies are used to sun, sea and surf. Therefore there's a bit of a culture shock when they end up in Wakefield which hasn't got any of these. New Zealand, on the other hand, is like Britain only with more sheep (68 million of them to be exact). For a start it rains there. They also drive on our side of the road and know what it's like to lose a test series.

Is Robbie Paul the one Peter Fox keeps telling people he signed? Yes, and it's true, although Peter neglects to mention that he then never bothered to pick him for the first team.

Other Rugby League brothers: Paul and David Hulme; Neil, Don and Peter Fox; Peter, Joe, Iva and Tea Ropati; Mike and Bernie Winters (just kidding).

Not to be confused with: Henry Paul (obviously), Junior Paul (London Broncos), Billy Paul (me and Mrs Jones), John Paul II (Vatican Blue Sox RLFC).

LANCE TODD
TROPHY
MAN OF THE MATCH

ROBBIE PAUL
FIRST
CHALLENGE CUP
HAT TRICK

KEEP ON RUNNING
WITH
THE BULLS

Spencer 96

"Put eet away Henri... Ze boys 'ave won a reprieve!"

"Don't jump Mr Chairman... The RFL said there's a slim chance we'll get into Super League next season!"

Bobbie Goulding

Description: Bad boy turned good guy.

Goulding... Goulding... I know that name. Oh yes, Rugby League's young tearaway. A combination of Gazza, a philosophy – free Eric Cantona and the rampaging Mongol hordes of Ghengh is Khan. No, you're thinking of the old Bobbie Goulding. We're talking about the new improved Bobbie, captain of St Helens and possessor of Britain's best kicking game.

What? You mean he's no longer synonymous with the words "volatile" and "incident"? The words used most now are "responsible" and "mature". Bobbie's always had the talent, now he's got the temperament to match.

That's a disappointment. I always liked a good Goulding incident.
You mean like the one in 1990 when Britain's youngest ever tourist was virtually deported from New Zealand after a punch – up in a restaurant? Or the way he was Young Player of the Year at Leeds one minute but leaving under a cloud the next? No, those days are gone. Bobbie may have managed to play for four different First Division teams by the time he was 22 but we reckon he'll be staying with St Helens for a while now.

Made a big impact at Knowsley Road has he? We can only point to the fact that when Saints played Bradford Bulls in the 1996 Challenge Cup final with him in the team they won 40-32, but when they played them again without him later the same season, they lost 50-22. At Wembley it was Bobbie's bombs that broke Bradford and helped destroy their 14 point lead and he would have probably won the Lance Todd Trophy if it hadn't gone to Robbie Paul. His performance definitely helped obliterate the memory of his last visit to the twin towers.

Are we talking "volatile" and "incident" again? Afraid so. When, in the Widnes v Wigan final in 1992, Richie Eyres became only the second man to be sent off in a Challenge Cup final Bobbie tried his best to become the third with a splendidly high tackle on Jason Robinson. Afterwards he was heard complaining: "My foul was much worse than Richie's. I should have been sent off as well".

Presumably the new Bobbie would never do that? No, although to be fair the old Bobbie could sometimes behave himself. He won winners medals with Wigan in 1990 and 1991 in incident – free finals. However, these days when Bobbie makes the headlines you can safely bet it's for the right reasons.

What's brought about this miraculous change? Bobbie puts it down to the influence of coaches such as Phil Larder and Eric Hughes and the fact that he's now a father. This, he claims, has calmed him down, and made him a better and wiser footballer, and all the evidence suggests he's right. Perhaps fatherhood should be recommended to Gazza, Eric Cantona and the rampaging Mongol hordes of Ghenghis Khan.

Not to be confused with: Bobbie Goulding Jnr (his son), Bobby Ball, Bobbie Gentry, William Golding.

Most likely to say: "Who wants a story before its up the wooden hill to Bedfordshire?"

Least likely to say: "Did you spill my pint? Right, outside now!"

THE ADVENTURES OF THE ED

by Andrew Griffiths "Rebel Rugby"

"Will was always fending off approaches from the other side!"

"At last... Something that looks almost edible!"

"Don't worry Ref... He'll not bite you!"

The Flat Cappers in Paris   by Wilde

SUBSCRIBE TO OPEN RUGBY

No Rugby League fan, or anybody who appreciates high-quality sports magazines, should miss

OPEN RUGBY

The monthly League magazine that brings you in-depth articles, features and informed comment from around the Rugby League world. PLUS, the most sparkling colour photographs you'll ever see.

OPEN RUGBY is the perfect magazine for Rugby League fans - in glorious full colour. Order your copy now!

Available by mail order
Send now for your sample copy: price £2.40 (inc. postage).

Or guarantee your copy for the next 12 issues by booking a postal subscription: price £29.00

International prices:
Europe £36, Zone 1 (airmail) £47, Zone 2 (airmail) £49, surface mail £34.

And every month **OPEN RUGBY** will be delivered through your letterbox.

Credit card order by phone
(or call us if you want to know more about *Open Rugby*)
0113-245-1560 or order by Fax: 0113-242-6255
Open Rugby, Munro House, York Street, Leeds LS9 8AP.

REBEL RUGBY

Order your copy from: Rebel Rugby, PO Box 81, Swansea SA1 6WF for just £1.00

THE TRUTH IS IN THERE

NEWS > VEIWS > AND ATTITUDE

ORDER YOUR COPY FROM "REBEL RUGBY" P.O.BOX 81, SWANSEA SA1 6WF FOR JUST £1.00

'EYUP OLD COCK!

HAVE YOU EVER FELT FRUSTRATED BECAUSE YOU DON'T FEEL REPRESENTED AS A SUPPORTER OF RUGBY LEAGUE?

DO YOU HAVE A POINT YOU'D LIKE TO MAKE, BUT DON'T FEEL THAT THERE'S ANYWHERE FOR YOU TO MAKE IT?

DO YOU WANT TO BE CONSULTED ABOUT THE WAY THE SUPER LEAGUE IS STRUCTURED AND RUN?

ARE YOU TIRED OF BEING LABELLED A FLATCAPPED WHIPPET FANCIER BY THE PRESS, JUST BECAUSE YOU LIKE RUGBY LEAGUE?

DO YOU WANT TO RECEIVE TGG!, THE WORLDS BEST RUGBY LEAGUE FANZINE, BEFORE ANYONE ELSE?

MAYBE YOU DO.

SO MAYBE YOU OUGHT TO JOIN THE R.L.S.A. NOW, AND BECOME PART OF THE ONLY NATIONAL RL SUPPORTERS ASSOCIATION IN THE U.K.

M.A.Wilde, 1995

OUR AGENDA :
- to democratically represent the views of members
- to campaign for supporters' opinions to be heard at all levels in the game
- to encourage friendship between supporters of all clubs and countries
- to work for the promotion and development of Rugby League, the greatest game of all.

For more information please write to :

THE RUGBY LEAGUE SUPPORTERS' ASSOCIATION
5 WESLEY STREET
CUTSYKE
CASTLEFORD
WEST YORKSHIRE : WF10 5HQ

Six years experience of working for supporters!